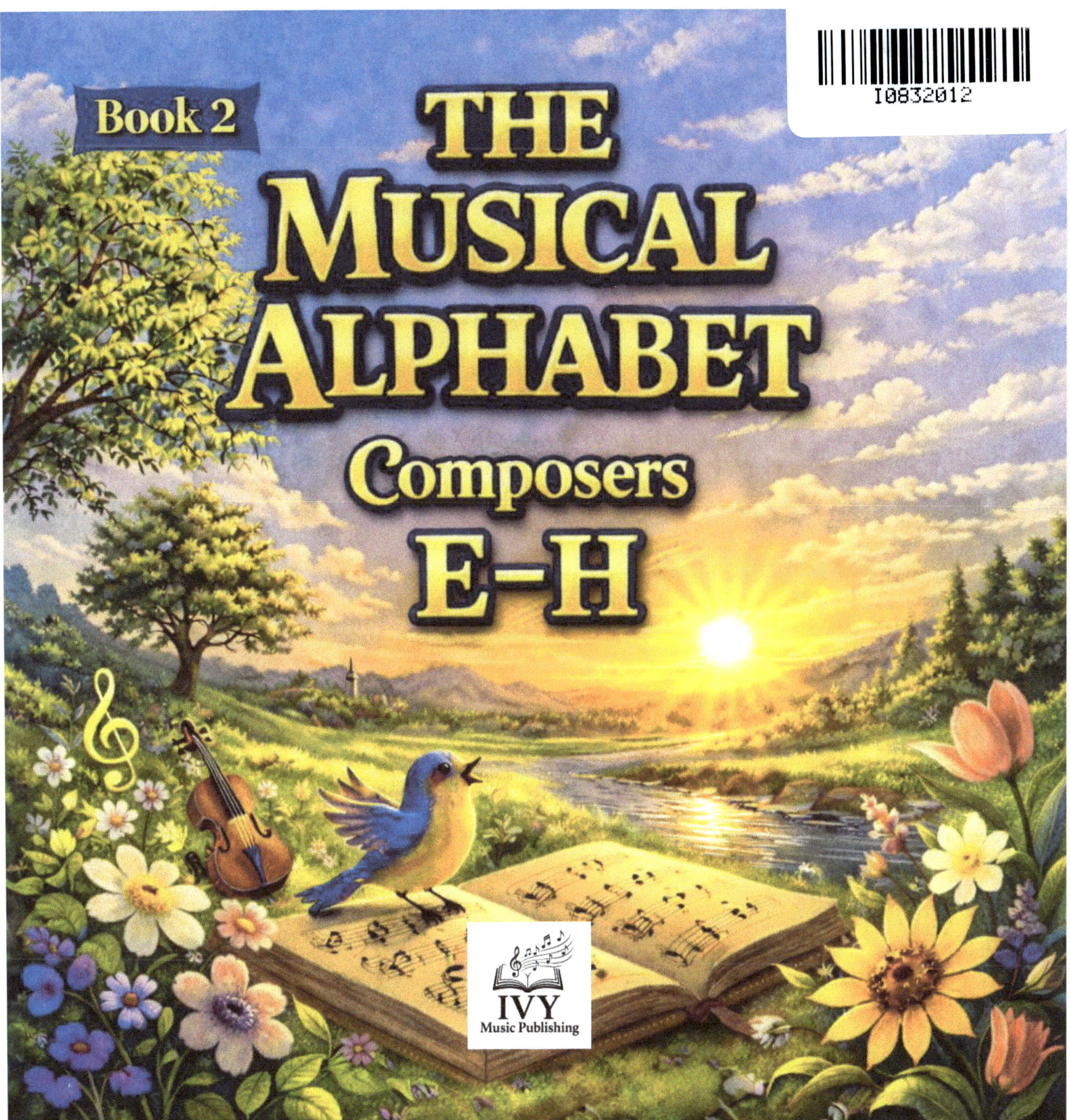
Book 2
THE MUSICAL ALPHABET
Composers
E–H
IVY
Music Publishing
I0832012

**The Musical Alphabet**
**Book 2: Composers E-H**



This edition is intended for informational and educational purposes.

All illustrations, texts, and musical materials are original works or are used with proper authorization.

Any resemblance to real people, living or deceased, is purely historical and educational in nature.

The author and publisher assume no responsibility for any consequences arising from the use of the information contained in this book.

Publisher: IVY Music Publishing
Author: Reena Young
United States of America

ISBN: 978-1-972314-01-2

*This series of books,*

**The Musical Alphabet,**

*is dedicated to my dear students.*

*Thank you for everything you have taught me!*

*With love,*

*Reena Young*

## Welcome to the wonderful world of music!

In this book, you will meet twelve great composers whose names begin with the letters E to H.

Their music comes from many countries and many centuries, yet it still inspires people all over the world.

Scan the QR codes, listen to the music, and discover how composers turn sounds into stories.

*Happy reading and listening!*

Contents:

## About the book:

It has long been known that classical music has a beneficial influence on a child's development. Yet behind these words lies not dry science, but a true and living miracle.

Music is alive.

It exists not only in the past, in textbooks, or in concert halls. It sounds around us every day — in films and cartoons, in theaters and games, at home by the piano, in headphones, and sometimes even in silence.

Classical music is not merely a beautiful sound. It is a living language of feelings, images, and moods that gently touches the human soul.

When a child listens to good music, tiny lights seem to turn on inside the brain. New connections are formed. Memory and attention grow. Imagination and speech develop. The ability to feel, to empathize, and to understand the world becomes deeper and richer.

The earlier music appears in a child's life, the deeper its roots grow. In early childhood, the foundations of future abilities are laid — intellectual, emotional, and creative.

That is why this series of books was created in a special way.

From the very beginning, it was conceived as a living musical ecosystem for children — an entire world where classical music becomes close, understandable, and beloved from the very first steps.

In these books, there is no dry listing of dates and complicated terms. Instead, the book invites the child into a space where composers become friends, musical works turn into stories, and listening becomes an exciting journey filled with discovery and joy.

Gradually, a natural interest in the world of beautiful, meaningful sounds emerges. This interest can support an active and curious mind throughout life, helping to preserve clarity of thought, inner culture, and a sense of wonder.

A special role in this process is played by the formation of taste. By hearing good music from early childhood, a child learns to distinguish the genuine from the superficial, to feel the expressiveness of melody, the warmth of harmony, and the power of rhythm.

Such taste becomes a quiet and reliable compass for a lifetime.

This Musical Alphabet was born from a simple but important idea: good music has no age. That is why different eras and styles live side by side in these books. Here you will meet great composers of the past as well as composers closer to our own time. All good music stands here as equal, because music speaks to people in the universal language of feelings.

From the very beginning, the author wished to avoid the impression that classical music is something distant, complicated, or meant only for a few specialists. Music can be beautiful, exciting, playful, mysterious, or solemn — and all of this is music.

Each book in this series may be opened at any page. You may begin with a composer whose name starts with the same letter as your child's name. You may start with music already familiar from a cartoon or a film. Or you may simply follow curiosity.

The books intentionally provide only a small amount of information about each composer. At this stage, it is enough to know the composer's name, recognize their music, and see their portraits. This is often enough for the first spark of interest to appear.

If a child later wishes to learn more, a vast world of knowledge is always open in libraries and on the Internet.

Some of the musical works presented in the book consist of several movements. For a first acquaintance, it is enough to listen to the first movement. The rest may be discovered later, if desired.

The books include links and QR codes leading to musical videos on YouTube. The author tried to select versions without advertisements, but unfortunately, this is not always possible. Therefore, it is recommended that adults help the child skip advertisements and remain nearby during listening.

These books do not aim to teach everything at once. Its purpose is much simpler and more important — **to begin a friendship with music**.

If, after this Alphabet, your child wishes to listen, play, ask questions, and discover more, then the books have fulfilled their most important purpose.

May this book become the first doorway into a great musical world — a world where every sound may turn into a small miracle.

With love for music and children,

Reena Young

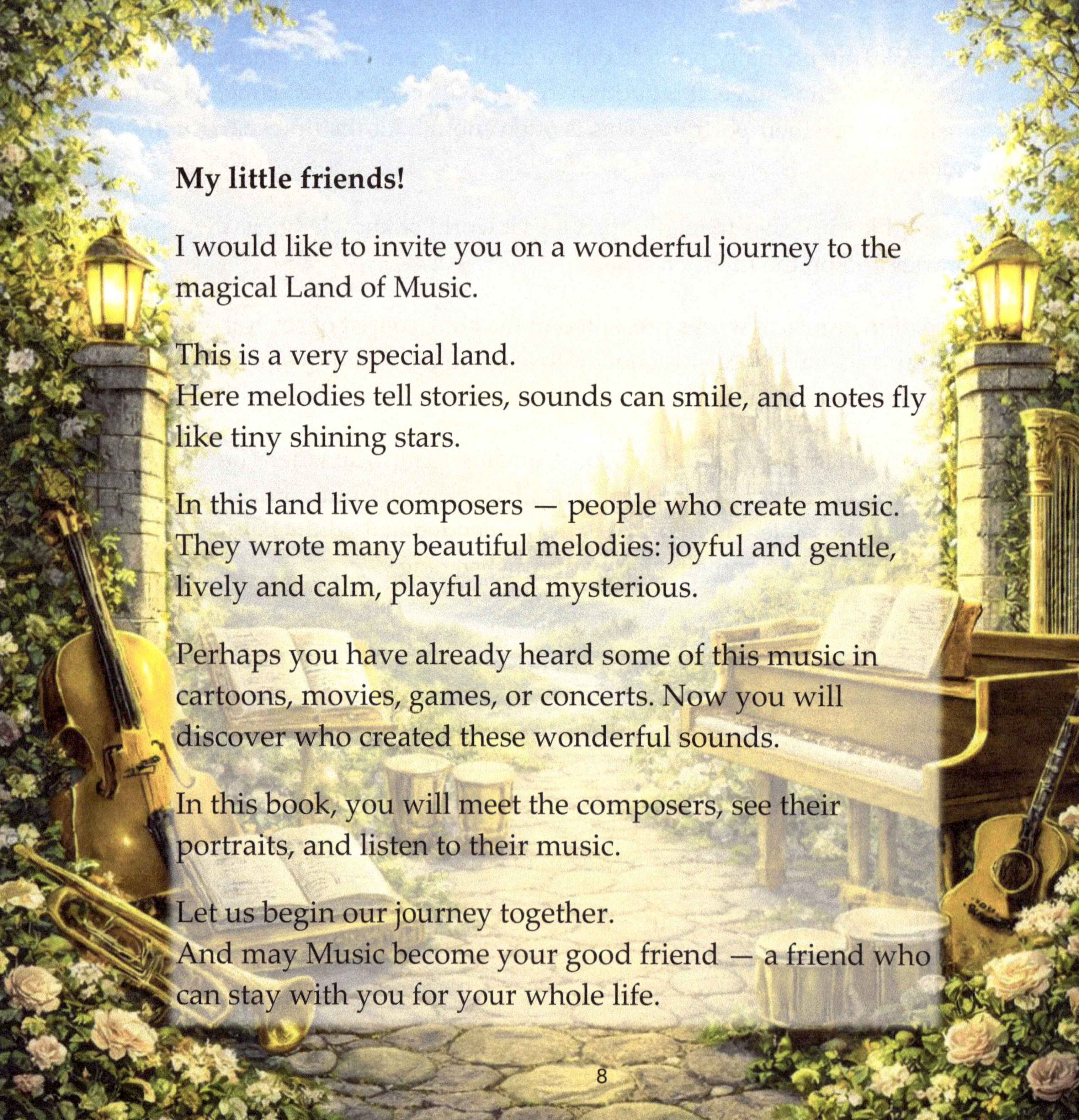

**My little friends!**

I would like to invite you on a wonderful journey to the magical Land of Music.

This is a very special land.
Here melodies tell stories, sounds can smile, and notes fly like tiny shining stars.

In this land live composers — people who create music. They wrote many beautiful melodies: joyful and gentle, lively and calm, playful and mysterious.

Perhaps you have already heard some of this music in cartoons, movies, games, or concerts. Now you will discover who created these wonderful sounds.

In this book, you will meet the composers, see their portraits, and listen to their music.

Let us begin our journey together.
And may Music become your good friend — a friend who can stay with you for your whole life.

# Elgar

## 1857 - 1934

**Edward Elgar** was an English composer. He was born in a small village near the city of **Worcester** in **England (United Kingdom)**.

Elgar wrote music for orchestra, violin, cello, and choir. His music often sounds noble, grand, and, at times, deeply emotional. One of his most famous works is his march, ***Pomp and Circumstance***, which is often played at important ceremonies and graduations.

Listen to the **Pomp and Circumstance March** performed by an orchestra conducted by the composer himself, **Edward Elgar**.

It is a very old recording — almost 100 years old!

https://www.youtube.com/results?search_query=elgar+pomp+and+circumstance+march+no.+3

# Enescu

## 1881 - 1955

**George Enescu** was one of the greatest musicians **Romania** has ever produced. He was born in the small village of **Liveni**, in northern **Romania**, and showed extraordinary musical talent from a very early age.

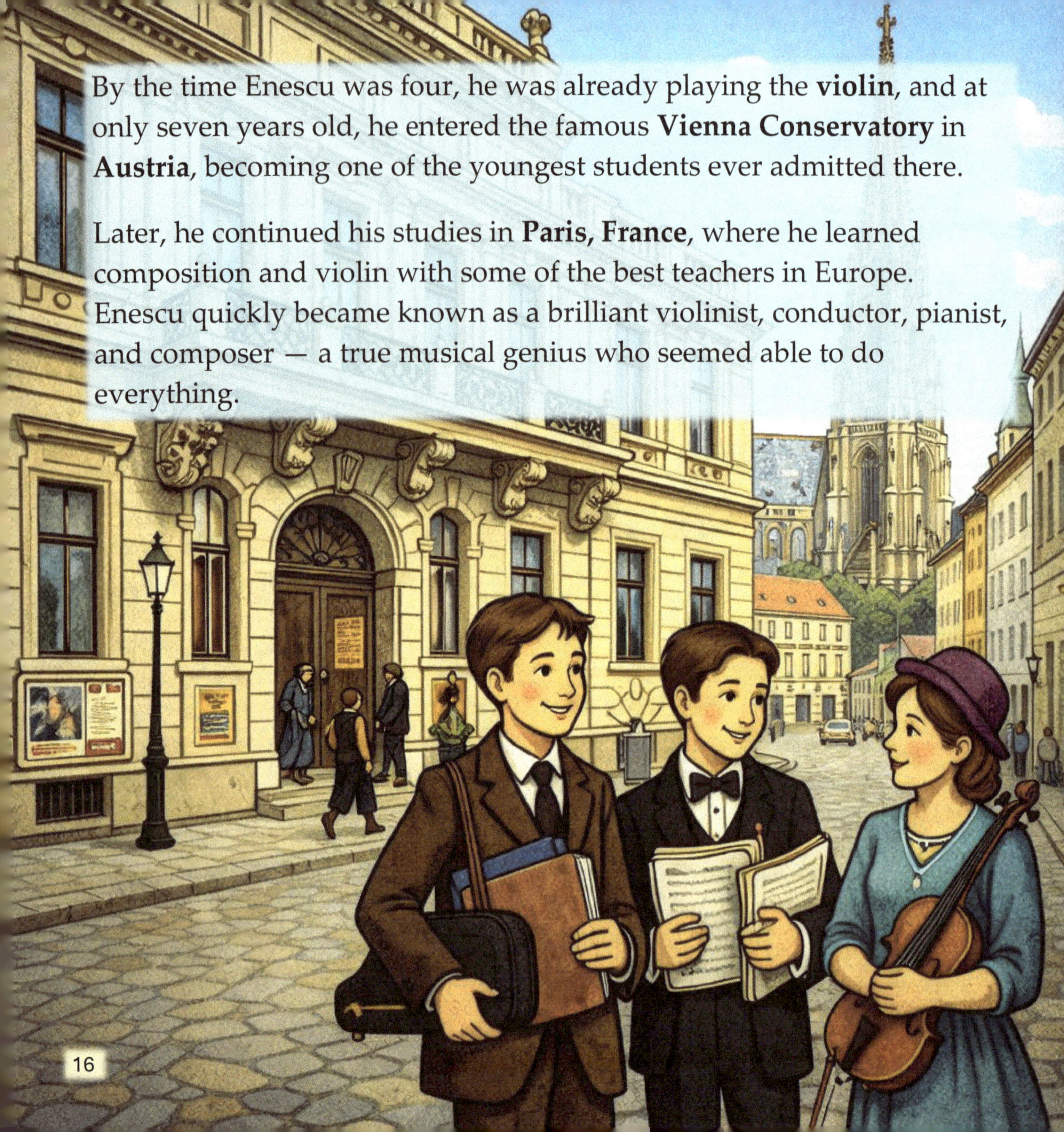

By the time Enescu was four, he was already playing the **violin**, and at only seven years old, he entered the famous **Vienna Conservatory** in **Austria**, becoming one of the youngest students ever admitted there.

Later, he continued his studies in **Paris, France**, where he learned composition and violin with some of the best teachers in Europe. Enescu quickly became known as a brilliant violinist, conductor, pianist, and composer — a true musical genius who seemed able to do everything.

His most famous works are the **Romanian Rhapsodies**, especially **Romanian Rhapsody No. 1**, which bursts with lively folk melodies and joyful dance rhythms from Romanian village traditions.

**The WDR Symphony Orchestra** from **Germany** performs Enescu's "Romanian Rhapsody No. 1" under the baton of the **Romanian** conductor **Cristian Măcelaru**. https://www.youtube.com/watch?v=cuU5sbXYAJ0

# Erik Satie

## 1866 - 1925

**Erik Satie** was a **French** composer and pianist.

He was born in **Honfleur, France**, and later lived most of his life in Paris.

As a young musician, he studied at the Paris Conservatory, but his teachers did not always understand his style.

He preferred simple melodies and calm, quiet music instead of dramatic, complicated pieces.

Satie became famous for his gentle piano works that sound peaceful, dreamy, and a little mysterious.

His music often feels light and thoughtful, as if it is speaking softly.

Satie influenced many later composers and helped shape modern music in the 20th century. His music is loved for its simplicity, elegance, and quiet beauty.

Listen to **Gymnopédie No. 1** performed by the **Georgian** pianist **Khatia Buniatishvili.**

A Gymnopédie is very calm, slow, and dreamy music.

It sounds like someone quietly walking in a garden at sunset or looking up at the stars.

https://www.youtube.com/watch?v=TL0xzp4zzBE&list=RDTL0xzp4zzBE&start_radio=1

# de Falla

## 1876 - 1946

**Manuel de Falla** was a **Spanish** composer who loved the sounds and colors of his homeland. He was born in the sunny city of **Cádiz, Spain**. From childhood, he studied piano and composition and dreamed of writing music that would feel truly Spanish.

De Falla's music is full of rhythm, passion, and the spirit of **flamenco.** Manuel de Falla helped bring the soul of Spain into concert halls around the world.

Listen to **Spanish Dance** performed by the young **Russian** violinist **Anna Savkina.**

https://www.youtube.com/watch?v=XjuOMNO3hjw&list=RDXjuOMNO3hjw&start_radio=1

# Fauré

## 1845–1924

**Gabriel Fauré** was a **French** composer, organist, pianist, and teacher. He was born in the town of **Pamiers** in southern **France**. As a child, he showed great musical talent and was sent to Paris to study at a special school for church musicians.

Later in life, Fauré became the director of the **Paris Conservatory**, where he taught and influenced a new generation of composers.

Fauré's music is calm, refined, and full of quiet beauty, and it remains loved by musicians and listeners around the world.

Listen to **Gabriel Fauré:** *Pavane* performed by the **Radio Philharmonic Orchestra of the Netherlands**.

A **pavane** is a very old, graceful court dance that was once performed at the courts of kings and nobles.

https://www.youtube.com/watch?v=HhiVulRw4tM

# Franck

## 1822 - 1890

**César Franck** was a composer, organist, and teacher of the Romantic era. He was born in **Liège (Belgium)** and later spent most of his life in **Paris, France**.

Franck became one of the greatest organists of his time. For many years, he served as the organist at the **Basilica of Sainte-Clotilde in Paris**, where his improvisations were renowned for their depth and beauty.

He was also an influential teacher at the **Paris Conservatory**. Many young composers admired him and called him **"Père Franck" (Father Franck)** because of his kindness and wisdom.

Listen to César Franck's ***Prelude, Fugue et Variation***, performed by cathedral organist **Matthias Maierhofer** from **Austria**.

https://www.youtube.com/watch?v=UJf5r1ZjwTY&list=RDUJf5r1ZjwTY&start_radio=1

# Gershwin

## 1898 - 1937

**George Gershwin** was an American composer and pianist. He was born in **Brooklyn, New York, USA**, but his parents were Jewish immigrants from the **Russian Empire**.

Gershwin loved two worlds of sound: classical music and jazz. Instead of choosing one, he decided to bring them together.

George Gershwin lived only 38 years, but in that short time, he changed American music forever. Today, his melodies are still performed in concert halls, jazz clubs, and movies all around the world.

Listen to **Clara's aria "Summertime"** from the opera ***Porgy and Bess.*** This excerpt is taken from the film of the same name.

[Porgy & Bess "Summertime" - YouTube]

# Gluck

## 1714 - 1787

**Christoph Willibald Gluck** was a **German** composer who lived in the 18th century. He wrote operas — musical stories in which the characters sing rather than speak.

The most famous opera composed by Gluck is ***Orfeo ed Euridice*** ("Orpheus and Eurydice").

It tells an ancient Greek story about Orpheus, a musician who loved his wife so much that he traveled to the Underworld to bring her back after

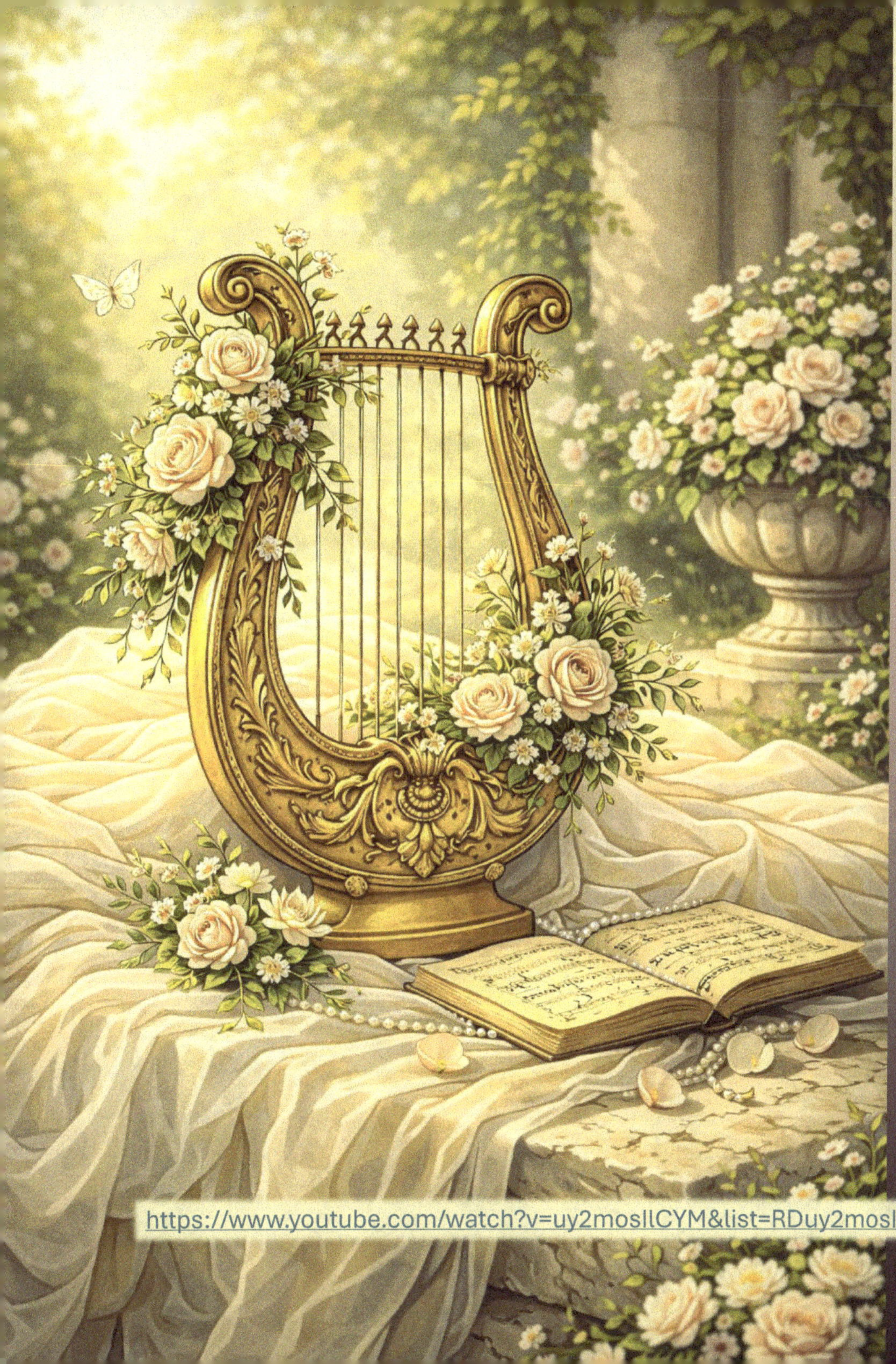

Listen to beautiful **"Melody"** from the opera ***Orfeo ed Euridice*** performed by **Zagreb Soloists** from **Croatia** and **Michael Martin Kofler**, flute, from **Austria**

https://www.youtube.com/watch?v=uy2mosIlCYM&list=RDuy2mosIlCYM

# Granados

## 1867 - 1916

**Enrique Granados** was a Spanish composer and pianist. He was born in **Lleida, Spain**, and later studied music in **Barcelona** and **Paris**.

The Granados' music is expressive, dramatic, and full of romantic feeling.

Granados loved Spanish culture, especially traditional dances and songs. Much of his music reflects the spirit of Spain. Many of Granados's works were arranged for guitar. Listen to **Spanish Dance No. 5** performed by **Kevin Enstrom** from Canada.

https://www.youtube.com/watch?v=ZqN7S2cJo-8&list=RDZqN7S2cJo-8&start_radio=1

# Grieg

## 1843 - 1907

**Edvard Grieg** was a **Norwegian** composer who deeply loved both music and the nature of his northern homeland, with its mountains, forests, and fjords.

Grieg wrote music that sounds like fairy tales, with themes of kings, trolls, and magical adventures.

One of Grieg's most famous musical fairy tales is called ***Peer Gynt***, named after its main character, who travels all over the world but eventually returns to his homeland.

He even visits the Hall of the Mountain King — and now you are going to watch a short video featuring the music **"In the Hall of the Mountain King."**

https://youtu.be/RIz3klPET3o?si=KwVuCCoLfvCIbMLS
https://www.youtube.com/watch?v=wl91UzszAh

# Handel

## 1685 - 1759

**George Frideric Handel** was born in **Germany** and later moved to **England**, where he wrote beautiful and festive music.

Handel wrote music for the theater and for great celebrations with large orchestras and choirs. His music sounds grand, joyful, and sometimes even magical. His most famous work is the oratorio ***Messiah,*** which is performed around the world at Christmas.

An oratorio is like an opera, but without costumes or stage sets. The "**Hallelujah**" chorus is the most famous part of it. Here it is performed by the **London Handel Orchestra and Choir** from the **United Kingdom**.

https://www.youtube.com/watch?v=n5pG6ve5HUI&list=RDn5pG6ve5HUI&start_radio=1

# Horner

## 1953 - 2015

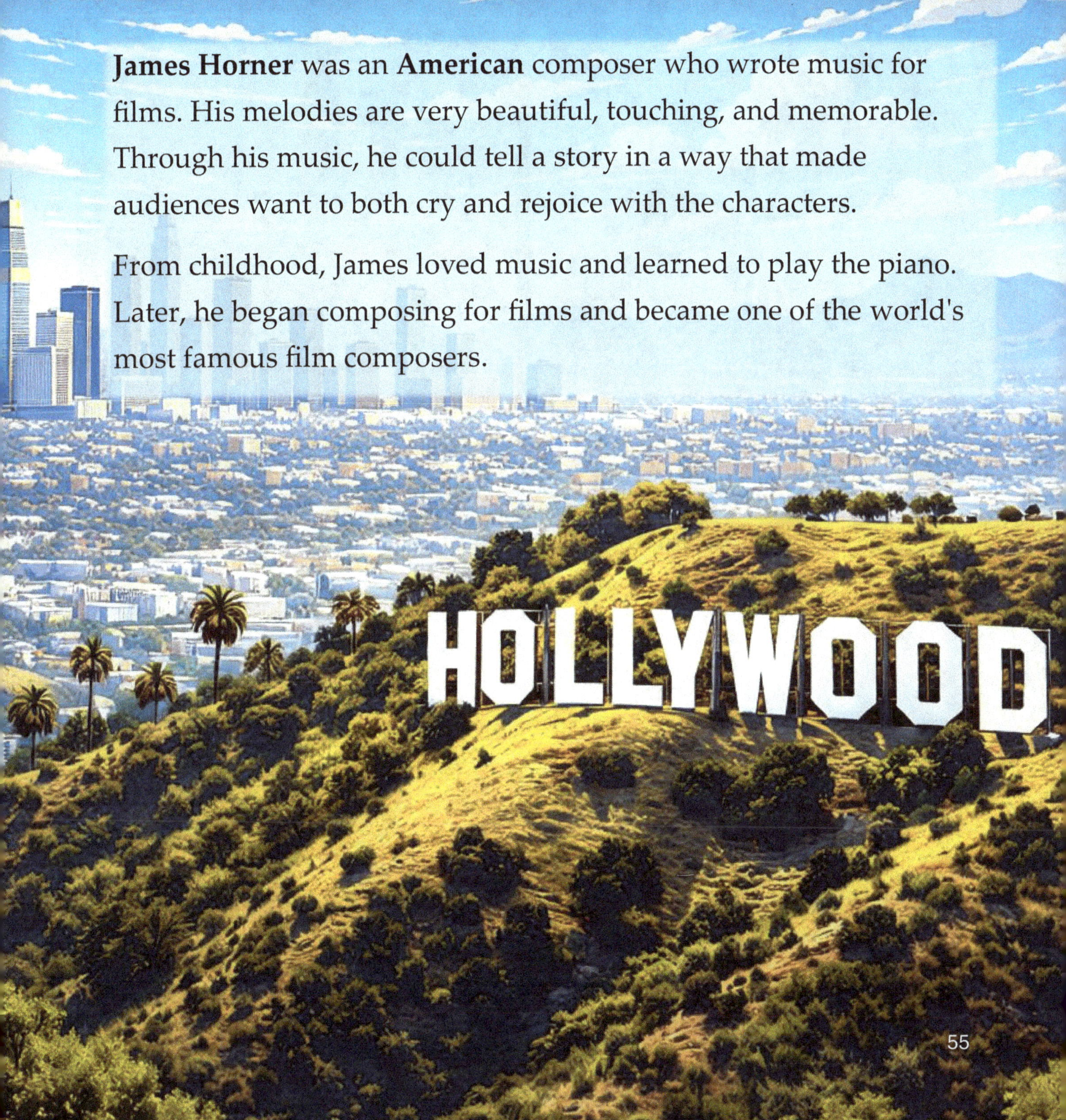


**James Horner** was an **American** composer who wrote music for films. His melodies are very beautiful, touching, and memorable. Through his music, he could tell a story in a way that made audiences want to both cry and rejoice with the characters.

From childhood, James loved music and learned to play the piano. Later, he began composing for films and became one of the world's most famous film composers.

Horner wrote music for more than 100 films.

His music often sounds like a great wave of emotion — sometimes gentle and dreamy, sometimes heroic and powerful.

For his work, he received several Academy Awards ("Oscars").

Listen to the **Film Symphony Orchestra** conducted by **Constantino Martínez-Orts** from **Spain**, performing **"The Ludlows"** from the movie ***Legends of the Fall.***

https://www.youtube.com/watch?v=L0gtDcbsly8

## Can you find them? (the answers are on the last page)

1. a trumpet
2. a piano
3. a fjord
4. a king and a queen
5. a letter F
6. a castle
7. the mountains
8. a fan
9. a baby
10. a set of drums
11. a letter E
12. a violin
13. a river
14. a sheep
15. a dancer
16. a church organ
17. an Eiffel Tower
18. a letter G
19. a guitar
20. New York City
21. A Mountain King
22. an American flag
23. an orchestra
24. a letter H
25. a HOLLYWOOD sign
26. a ship

## Musical Questions (the answers are on the last page)

1. Which composer wrote music for movies?

2. Which composer lived in Romania?

3. Which composer brought together jazz and classical music?

4. Which composers wrote music for operas?

5. How many composers were born in Spain?

6. Which composer wrote music inspired by northern fairy tales?

7. Which composers lived in England (United Kingdom)

## Appendix 1.

## *Additional works to enjoy on YouTube.*

1. The best of **Elgar**

https://youtu.be/TK5samL9ECI?si=ZpTosptZFGv8uKth

1. 

2. The best of **Enescu**

https://youtu.be/DdgRjFSR_oM?si=40PsJUsofYF_dFy7

2. 

**3.** The best of **Erik Satie**

https://youtube.com/playlist?list=PL_qM1lclHDwXC_5s0HeRmZMf74enIzL7m&si=AMkemWz3-C4k-Mu8

3. 

4. The best of **de Falla**

https://youtu.be/p0Yd3W6cKGA?si=4_42uDEX6EeiLIht.

4. 

## 5. More of **de Falla**

https://youtube.com/playlist?list=PLa1rC97wRkZiSgJilHboUs-VYF0gdwvQr&si=S5O6updcAqY94dVD

5.

## 6. The best of **Fauré**

https://youtube.com/playlist?list=PLfjK3WmtgQN593T8BjkBKSNv4n6OcGhnB&si=j9okBnGhWig3MlFG

6.

## 7. The best of **Frank**

https://youtu.be/DtRt1tBAzr4?si=liVtXm7PgrBmHs5O.

7.

## 8. The best of **Gershwin**

A https://www.youtube.com/watch?v=mM-K2xVFyk0

B https://youtu.be/oQdeTbUDCiw?si=8_yDcO3Q9yEAZZ6E

C https://youtu.be/lGpMLoFyjwA?si=jLLzzZxEOqTW1jrK

## 9. The best of **Gluck**

https://youtube.com/playlist?list=PLXqvnMAThLNlD7wpVK4OvypA6wvY-KeWm&si=-kNRngr1LMkZfz8i

## 10. The best of **Granados**

A https://www.youtube.com/watch?v=CrRRa-tMpBk

B https://youtu.be/ZqN7S2cJo-8?si=tnJ3bMrxKs0bb1eo

## 11. The best of **Grieg**

https://youtu.be/tnJzu0arFsU?si=k5tT1z37IwXuz9Qm

## 12. The best of **Handel**

https://youtu.be/heHJukTDHvw?si=0I2eKPwi7hPjwSpC

## 13. The best of **Horner**

https://youtube.com/playlist?list=PLO6S2qKFLcloW_HZR4JOsX07bbLbosPrg&si=T0XW7BYDi351CLvu

## Appendix 2. More Music to Explore

If you enjoyed discovering these composers, here are more beautiful pieces you can listen to.
Try to find them on YouTube and choose the performance you like most.

**Edward Elgar**

• *Salut d'Amour*
— warm and lyrical, like a gentle love song

• *Chanson de Matin*
— bright and light, like a fresh morning

• *Enigma Variations – Nimrod*
— calm and noble, slowly growing in sound

**George Enescu**

• *Romanian Rhapsody No. 2*
— more calm and flowing, with a lyrical mood

• *Cantabile et Presto*
— begins gently, then becomes fast and energetic

• *Impressions d'enfance (The Fiddler)*
— expressive and imaginative, like a musical story

**Erik Satie**

• *Gnossienne No. 1*
— free and slightly mysterious, without a strict rhythm

- *Je te veux*

— light and graceful, like a gentle dance

- *Gymnopédie No. 3*

— slow and peaceful, with a soft, flowing melody

**Manuel de Falla**

- *Ritual Fire Dance (El amor brujo)*

— rhythmic and intense, like a magical dance

- *Seven Spanish Folk Songs – Nana*

— soft and gentle, like a lullaby

- *El sombrero de tres picos – Dance of the Miller*

— lively and playful, full of character

**Gabriel Fauré**

- *Sicilienne, Op. 78*

— light and graceful, with a gentle rhythm

- *Après un rêve*

— warm and expressive, like a dream remembered

- *Berceuse, Op. 16*

— soft and flowing, like a cradle song

**César Franck**

- *Panis Angelicus*

— peaceful and lyrical, like a quiet prayer

*Symphony in D minor (2nd movement)*
— calm and rich, with a singing melody

**George Gershwin**

• *An American in Paris*
— bright and energetic, like a walk through a busy city

• *Prelude No. 1*
— bold and rhythmic, with a jazzy character

• *Fascinating Rhythm*
— lively and playful, with a clear, driving pulse

**Christoph Willibald Gluck**

• *Overture to Orfeo ed Euridice*
— clear and balanced, with a calm opening

• *Che farò senza Euridice*
— simple and expressive, like a heartfelt song

**Enrique Granados**

• *Oriental (Spanish Dance No. 2)*
— gentle and flowing, with a dreamy mood

• *Goyescas – Intermezzo*
— rich and lyrical, with a singing melody

• *Danza lenta (from Danzas españolas)*
— calm and expressive, with a soft, reflective character

**Edvard Grieg**

• *Morning Mood (Peer Gynt Suite)*
— bright and peaceful, like sunrise

• *Lyric Pieces – Arietta*
— simple and tender, like a quiet thought

• *Holberg Suite – Gavotte*
— lively and elegant, with a dance-like rhythm

**George Frideric Handel**

• *Water Music – Suite (Hornpipe)*
— bright and festive, like music for a royal celebration

• *Water Music – Air*
— calm and elegant, with a smooth, flowing melody

• *Arrival of the Queen of Sheba (Solomon)*
— lively and graceful, full of light and movement

**James Horner**

• *My Heart Will Go On (Titanic)*
— gentle and emotional, with a memorable melody

• *For the Love of a Princess (Braveheart)*
— warm and expressive, with a noble feeling

• *A Gift of a Thistle (Braveheart)*
— soft and lyrical, like a quiet reflection

**Our journey through the Land of Music continues.**
**In the next book, new composers and new musical stories are waiting for you.**

# COLLECT THE MUSICAL ALPHABET SERIES

*Each book opens a new door into the world of music.*

BOOK 1 Composers A – D:

Albéniz
Albinoni
Anderson
Bach
Beethoven
Brahms
Chopin
Clara Schumann
Debussy
Delibes
Dukas
Dvořák

- - - - - - - - - - - - - - - - - - - - - - - - - - - - - - - - - - - - - - - -

BOOK 2 Composers E – H:

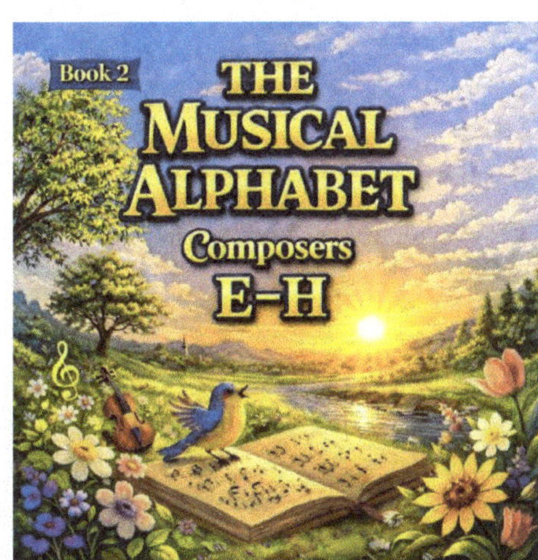


Elgar
Enescu
Erik Satie
De Falla
Fauré
Franck
Gershwin
Gluck

Granados

Grieg

Handel

Horner

- - - - - - - - - - - - - - - - - - - - - - - - - - - - - - - - - - - - - - -

BOOK 3 Composers I – L: Ibert

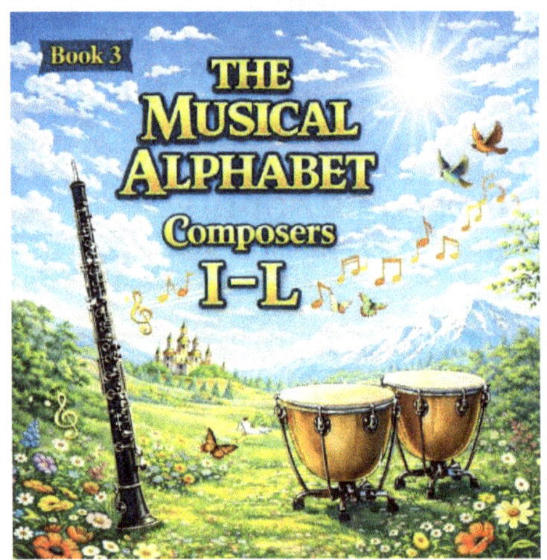


Irving Berlin

Ives

Jean Sibelius

Joseph Haydn

Jules Massenet

Kálmán

Kabalevsky

Khachaturian

Kreisler

Lehár

Liszt

- - - - - - - - - - - - - - - - - - - - - - - - - - - - - - - - - - - - - - -

BOOK 4 Composers M – P:

Mancini

Mendelssohn

Milhaud

Morricone

Mozart
Nino Rota
Offenbach
Ogiński
Pachelbel
Paganini
Prokofiev
Puccini

---

BOOK 5 Composers Q – S:

*Coming in 2026*

Quilter
Rachmaninoff
Ravel
Rimsky-Korsakov
Rossini
Saint-Saëns
Schumann
Shore
Shostakovich
Sousa
Strauss
Stravinsky

BOOK 6 Composers T – W:

*Coming in 2026*

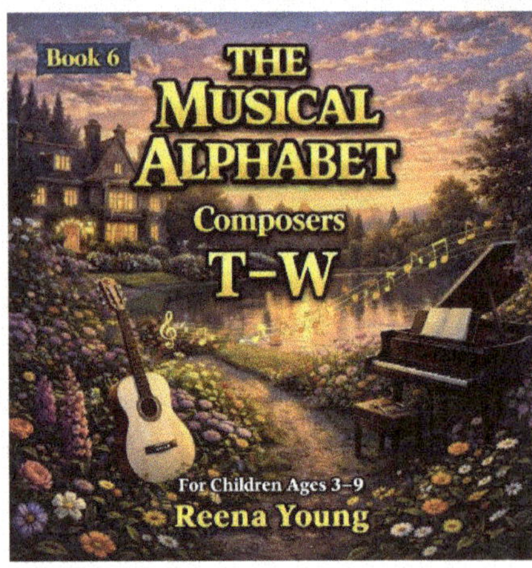


Tartini
Tchaikovsky
Telemann
Torelli
Vanhal
Verdi
Villa-Lobos
Vivaldi
Wagner
Webber
Wieniawski
Williams

Bonus: Ukrainian music

---

BOOK 7 Composers X – Z:

*Coming in 2026*

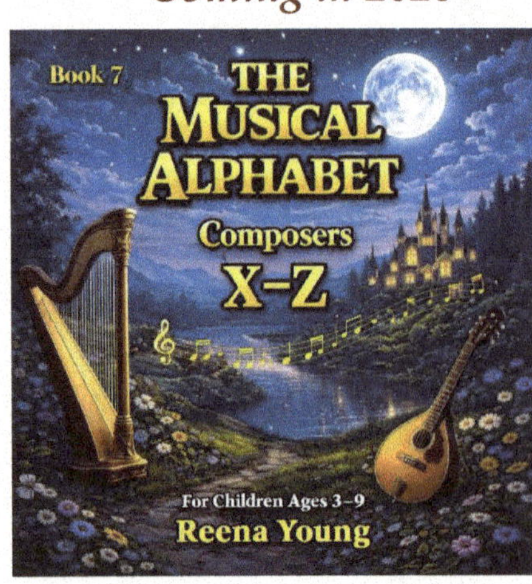


Xaver Scharwenka
Xian Xinghai
Yanni
Yamada
Yoko Kanno
Ysaÿe
Zdeněk Fibich
Zélenka
Zieleński
Zelter

Zimbalist
Zimmer

- - - - - - - - - - - - - - - - - - - - - - - - - - - - - - - - - - - - - - - - - - - - -

## BOOK 8 Musical Instruments

- - - - - - - - - - - - - - - - - - - - - - - - - - - - - - - - - - - - - - - - - - - - -

## BOOK 9 Genres and Forms of Music

- - - - - - - - - - - - - - - - - - - - - - - - - - - - - - - - - - - - - - - - - - - - -

## BOOK 10 The Great Performers

- - - - - - - - - - - - - - - - - - - - - - - - - - - - - - - - - - - - - - - - - - - - -

## BOOK 11 Music for the Screen

- - - - - - - - - - - - - - - - - - - - - - - - - - - - - - - - - - - - - - - - - - - - -

## BOOK 12 The Ages of Music

# Appendix 3.
## Glossary

### Adagio
A musical term meaning *slow and calm*. Music played adagio feels peaceful and expressive.

### Ballerina
A female ballet dancer. She performs graceful dances on stage, often wearing special pointe shoes.

### Ballet
A type of theater performance where a story is told through dance and music.

### Ballet variation
A short solo dance in a ballet that shows the dancer's skill and character.

### Basilica
A large and important church building. Many famous organs and sacred musical works are performed in basilicas.

### Cello
A large string instrument played with a bow. It has a deep, warm sound and is usually played while sitting.

### Chamber orchestra
A small orchestra with fewer musicians than a symphony orchestra. It usually performs in smaller halls.

### *Choir*
A group of singers who perform together, often in churches, concert halls, or opera productions.

**Composer**
A person who writes music.

**Concerto**
A musical piece in which a solo instrument plays alongside an orchestra.

**Conductor**
The person who leads the orchestra and helps all the musicians play together.

**Conservatory**
A special school where students study music, singing, and musical instruments.

**Ensemble**
A small group of musicians playing music together.

**Flamenco** is a style of music and dance from Spain, full of strong emotions and rhythm.

**Flute**
A wind instrument that makes sound when the player blows across a small opening.

**Fugue**
A musical composition where the same theme is repeated and developed by different voices or instruments.

**Guitar**
A string instrument that is usually played by plucking or strumming the strings.

**Harpsichord**
An early keyboard instrument from the Baroque period. Its strings are plucked rather than struck, as on a piano.

**Mazurka**
A lively Polish dance in triple rhythm.

**Opera**
A theatrical performance in which the story is sung rather than spoken.

**Operetta**
A lighter and shorter type of opera, often with funny or romantic stories.

**Organ**
A large keyboard instrument usually found in churches. It produces sound using air and pipes.

**Oratorio**
A large musical work for orchestra, choir, and solo singers, usually based on a religious story.

**Piano**
A keyboard instrument where strings are struck by small hammers when the keys are pressed.

**Polonaise**
A stately Polish dance in triple time.

**Prelude**
A short musical piece that introduces a larger work or sets a mood.

**Prodigy**
A child with extraordinary talent, especially in music.

**Rhapsody**
A free and expressive musical composition, often inspired by folk melodies.

**Rhythm**
The pattern of beats in music — the way sounds are organized in time.

**Romance**
A lyrical and expressive musical piece, often gentle and emotional.

**Sonata**
A musical composition, usually written for one instrument or a small group of instruments.

**Suite**
A collection of short musical pieces played one after another.

**Symphonic orchestra**
A very large orchestra with strings, woodwinds, brass, and percussion instruments.

**Symphonic poem**
An orchestral piece that tells a story or describes an idea, a poem, or a scene.

**Symphony**
A large musical work for orchestra, usually made of several movements.

**Toccata**
A fast and brilliant musical piece that shows the performer's skill.

**Variation (music)**
A musical form where a theme is repeated several times, but each time it is changed in a new way.

**Viola**
A string instrument slightly larger than a violin, with a deeper sound.

**Violin**
A small string instrument played with a bow.

**Did your child enjoy this musical journey?**

**The last question: which composer(s) do you like the most?**

---

I would truly love to hear your thoughts. Your review helps other children and parents discover this book and continue their journey into the world of music.

For your convenience, simply scan the QR code below to go directly to the review page on Amazon or use the link.

Thank you for being part of this story.

With love,
Reena Young

https://a.co/d/07fuLb5j

**Can you find them?**

1. Pages 12
2. 20, 36
3. 47, 48
4. 12
5. 22, 26, 30
6. 27, 39, 40
7. 15, 27, 39, 47, 48, 57
8. 22, 25
9. 37
10. 36
11. 10, 14, 18
12. 14, 16, 17, 20, 52
13. 9, 11, 19, 27, 28, 31, 39, 40, 57
14. 15
15. 17, 24, 44
16. 32, 33
17. 28
18. 34, 38, 42
19. 22, 24, 42, 44, 45
20. 35
21. 49
22.34, 35, 55
23. 52
24. 50, 54
25. 55
26. 56

**Musical questions:**

1. James Horner
2. George Enescu
3. George Gershwin
4. Christoph Willibald Gluck and George Gershwin
5. Two: Manuel de Falla and Enrique Granados
6. Edward Grieg
7. Edward Elgar

## The other books by Reena Young

**Skillful Little Fingers** is a preparatory piano method designed to help young students feel confident and at ease at the keyboard from the very beginning.

Through carefully structured exercises, children become familiar with both white and black keys early on, reducing fear and building natural coordination. Special attention is given to black-key groups, Chopin's Position, B major, and chromatic preparation, so that when music theory appears later, the hands already feel at home.

The book is intentionally flexible. It is not intended to replace any method chosen by the teacher, but rather to complement and enrich existing piano instruction. Exercises can be integrated freely into lessons, adapted to individual students, and used alongside any curriculum.

Designed for young hands and developing minds, **Skillful Little Fingers** supports a calm, confident, and joyful start at the piano.

**Skillful Little Fingers** – Book II continues the journey toward confident, natural piano technique.

This book builds on the foundation established in Book I and gently expands the student's experience across the keyboard. Scales, patterns, and coordinated movements are introduced in a clear and practical way, without rushing into abstract theory.

One important goal of this book is to help the hands feel comfortable on both white and black keys. Through consistent finger patterns and carefully designed exercises, the keyboard becomes familiar rather than intimidating.

The material in this book is not meant to replace any existing piano method. Instead, it is designed to complement the teacher's chosen approach and support technical development alongside repertoire.

Skillful Little Fingers focuses on what matters most at this stage:

relaxed hands, balanced movement, and growing confidence at the keyboard.

www.ingramcontent.com/pod-product-compliance
Lightning Source LLC
LaVergne TN
LVHW081420110826
845149LV00010B/1809

* 9 7 8 1 9 7 2 3 1 4 0 1 2 *